PUPPIES

JEN BESEL

BLACK
RABBIT
BOOKS

Bolt Jr. is published by Black Rabbit Books
P.O. Box 3263, Mankato, Minnesota, 56002.
www.blackrabbitbooks.com
Copyright © 2020 Black Rabbit Books

Michael Sellner, designer; Omay Ayres, photo researcher

Names: Besel, Jennifer M., author.
Title: Puppies / by Jen Besel.
Description: Mankato, Minnesota : Black Rabbit Books,
[2020] | Series: Bolt Jr. baby animals | Includes
bibliographical references and index. | Audience: Age 6-8. |
Audience: K to Grade 3.
Identifiers: LCCN 2019001241 (print) | LCCN 2019002750
(ebook) | ISBN 9781623101480 (e-book) |
ISBN 9781623101428 (library binding) |
ISBN 9781644660980 (paperback)
Subjects: LCSH: Puppies—Juvenile literature.
Classification: LCC SF426.5 (ebook) | LCC SF426.5 .B48
2020 (print) | DDC 636.7/07—dc23
LC record available at https://lccn.loc.gov/2019001241

Printed in the United States. 5/19

Contents

CHAPTER 1

A Hungry Baby

A little puppy **wobbles** as it learns to walk. It trips over its sister. Then the two puppies wrestle. But they soon need their mother. They're sleepy and hungry!

wobble: to move from side to side in a shaky way

newborn puppy ◀ ⋯⋯⋯ **WEIGHT COMPARISON**

less than 2 pounds
(1 kilogram)

Growing Fast

Newborn puppies can't see or hear. But they can smell! Their mothers stay with them. They keep the pups safe. Puppies start to see and hear in about two weeks.

▶ 2 cans of soup
2 pounds
(1 kg)

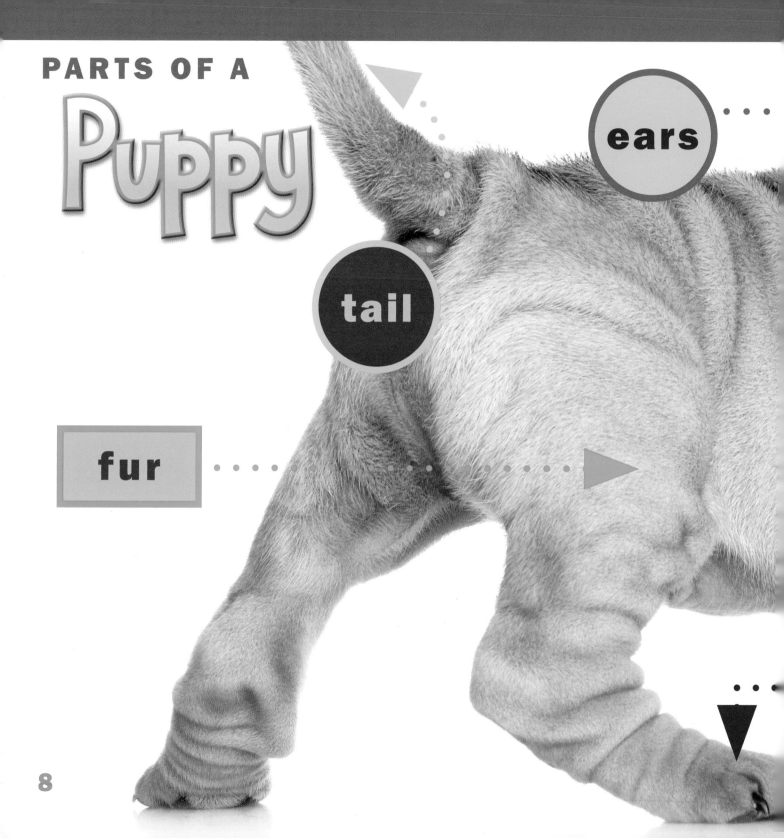

PARTS OF A

PuPPy

ears

tail

fur

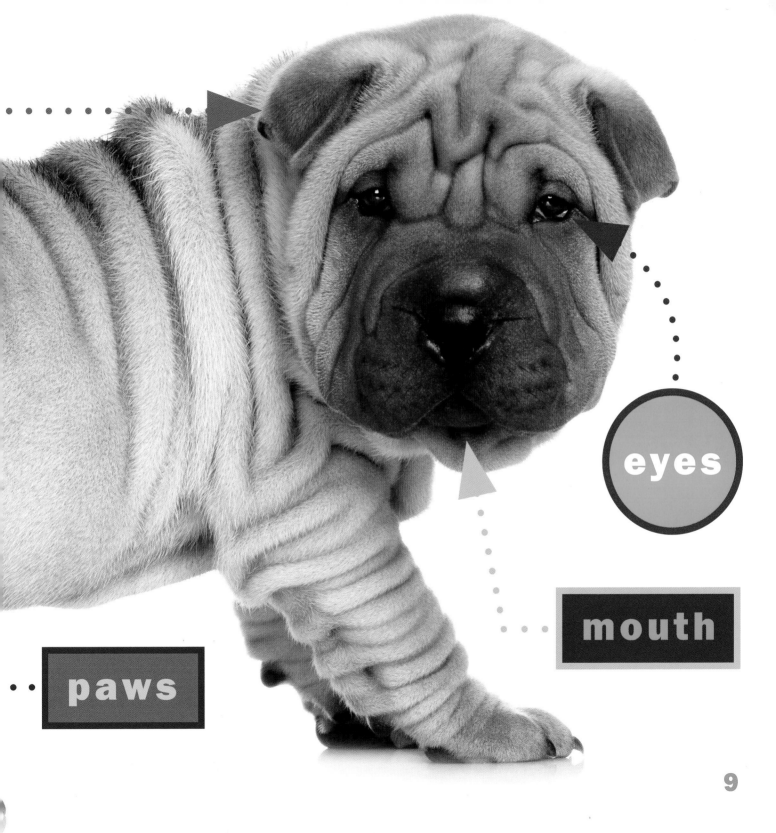

eyes

mouth

paws

9

CHAPTER 2

Food and Homes

Puppies are playful **explorers**. They get hungry. At first, they drink their mothers' milk. As they grow, their teeth come in. Then they can eat **solid** food.

explorer: one who searches and discovers

solid: not liquid or gas

FACT
Puppy teeth are small and sharp.

A Warm Home

Pet puppies need safe, warm homes. They need beds and food bowls. They also need toys to **chew** on.

chew: to crush with teeth

Top 5 Countries with the Most Pet Dogs

United States

Brazil

14

Russia

Japan

China

15

CHAPTER 3

Growing Up

Puppies learn a lot as they grow.

They learn to clean themselves.

They learn to run, chase, and jump.

They also learn to watch for danger.

FACT

Puppies sleep up to 20 hours a day.

Leaving Mom

At about three months old, puppies can care for themselves. They can leave their mothers.

Most dogs are fully grown by their first birthdays. They can soon have puppies of their own.

Big and Small

4

200

Some dogs weigh as little as 4 pounds (2 kg). Others are more than 200 pounds (91 kg).

Bonus Facts

Puppies lose their baby teeth.

A dog was the first animal in space.

There are up to 344 kinds of dogs.

Every dog's **noseprint** is different.

noseprint: a pattern of marks made by pressing an animal's nose to a surface

READ MORE/WEBSITES

Heim, Alastair. *The Great Puppy Invasion*. New York: Clarion Books, Houghton Mifflin Harcourt, 2017.

Lynch, Annabelle. *Dogs and Puppies*. Animals and Their Babies. Mankato, MN: Smart Apple Media, 2017.

Suen, Anastasia. *Puppies*. Baby Farm Animals. Mankato, MN: Amicus, 2019.

Dogs! Learning about Dog Facts for Kids
www.youtube.com/
watch?v=_0F7wFPRBmY&vl=en

Fun Dog Facts for Kids
www.sciencekids.co.nz/sciencefacts/
animals/dog.html

Fun Facts on Dogs and Puppies
www.fun-facts.org.uk/animals/animals-
dogs.htm

GLOSSARY

chew (CHEW)—to crush with teeth

explorer (ek-SPLOR-uhr)—one who searches and discovers

noseprint (NOHZ-print)—a pattern of marks made by pressing an animal's nose to a surface

solid (SAH-lid)—not liquid or gas

wobble (WAH-buhl)—to move from side to side in a shaky way

INDEX